QUAILS 101

THE MOST ASKED QUESTIONS AND ANSWERS ON QUAIL FARMING

Special Dedication

To every quail farmer

Acknowledgments

I am most appreciative of the many people who offered invaluable views, ideas, and support towards the making of this book.

To Arnold, Steve, Anne, David, Rachael, Moses, Amos, Emmaculate and Dr. Ruth, thank you all, and may the almighty God bless you richly.

Finally, but most important, I thank God for the gift of life, inspiration, knowledge and for His endless blessings upon my life. Indeed, great is His faithfulness. His grace, love and mercy, surely endures forever!

Contents

Quail Eggs

Question

My Japanese quail has just laid an egg with pure white eggshell. What could be the reason?

Answer

Healthy Japanese quail normally lay spotted eggs. The eggshell has patches of black, brown, or sometimes blue colors. Equally, there are emerging mutants of Japanese quail which can lay eggs with white shells. However, if the hen has been laying spotted eggs but suddenly laid a white-shelled egg, it could be possible its pigment gland may have malfunctioned. Consequently, the best remedy would be to consult a trained and experienced poultry vet for right diagnosis and treatment of the affected hen.

Question

I have been keeping female quails for close to three months now but they are yet to lay any egg. What could be the problem?

Answer

Fascinatingly, it is true that quail can reach egg laying stage but still fail to lay eggs. To stimulate such birds to start laying eggs, ensure that their accommodation is free from noise and any form of disturbance from pets and rodents which might distract them. Equally, you'll need to increase the amount of calcium in their feeds, provide them with plenty of clean, freshwater for drinking, and expose them to light (natural or artificial) for extended hours; 14-16 hours each 24 hours is most ideal.

Question
How long do quail eggs take to hatch?

Answer
This depends on the type of quail breed you are raising. Naturally, quail eggs from common breeds such as the Japanese quail do take between 16-18 days from the day of incubation to hatch. However, there are emerging quail mutants whose eggs may take 14 to 15 days from the day of incubation to hatch.

Question
How can I stimulate higher production of eggs from my flock?

Answer
To stimulate higher production of eggs from the hens, you'll need to exercise the below:

- Raise a healthy flock free from disease infection.
- The hens should be young yet mature with known genetical ability to realize high production efficiency.
- Feed the hens on nutritious and well balanced feeds with plenty of clean and freshwater availed to them for drinking.
- Ensure correct amount of lighting for extended period of time (usually 14 hours each 24 hours).

- The hens must be raised under noise-free and disturbance free environment. Such distractions hinder their egg laying potential.

How can I tell that a quail egg is fertile?

It can be a tough task for an average quail keeper to tell a fertile quail egg from an infertile one. However, there should be no cause for alarm. To start you off, you can use the below three observable signs to tell right away an infertile egg:

- Cracks on the eggshell.
- Absence of yolk or presence of double yolk. This can be detected via candling
- Dark spots/blood spots/ or bloody ring around or in the yolk. These too can be detected through candling.

The first step to guarantee fertility of a quail egg is through correct pairing of the birds, in the ratio of one male to a maximum of three females. Onwards, on the seventh day of incubation, you can candle the eggs. Using a candling lamp, a fertile egg will show a reddish embryo, while an infertile one will show a clear embryo.

But if unsure about the colors on the seventh day, you can again candle the eggs on the 13th or 14th day of incubation. If the chick is absent, you will see a larger section of the egg containing a clear embryo, with a tiny space containing air. But if the chick is present, the embryo will appear dark, or the light may not be able to penetrate through the eggshell.

Question

Is it advisable to purchase already egg laying birds for commercial egg-production?

Answer

Yes you can, but first, you need to put the below into consideration:

When quail begin to lay eggs, it is never easy for an average keeper to tell their exact ages. It is therefore, possible to acquire birds in their third year of egg laying, or even birds approaching their egg-laying-menopause, if the purchase is made at the egg-laying stage. It is interesting to note that quails do slow down and would eventually stop putting on more weight as their approach maturity. Therefore, just by looking at their sizes, at times, it would not be easy to be able to tell their exact ages.

It is equally proven through research that a number of female birds do lay eggs consistently within their first years. However, in the subsequent years, their rate of egg laying may begin to slow down, or may become inconsistent and eventually disappear as they age. Did you know that an egg laid by a three-year-old domesticated quail may be infertile? This may result into massive waste of resources by any farmer on such birds if the intention is to incubate their eggs.

It is advisable that for a more productive quail farming venture, especially quail farming for commercial egg production, a quail farmer should aim to acquire birds which are utmost five weeks old. At that stage, their vitality and productiveness can be guaranteed. However, if a farmer has the capacity to hatch the eggs, then that would be the most recommended route.

Question

What are some of the characteristics of an infertile quail egg, or a quail egg unfit for human consumption?

Answer

- ## Soft eggshells or thin eggshells

  Soft eggshell may be a resultant of the hen prematurely laying the egg. It symbolizes lack of proper calcification which ought to have taken place in the hen's shell gland. On the other hand, thin eggshells may symbolize disease infection, or nutritional deficiency. You should consult a properly trained poultry vet to help you diagnose and treat the affected bird.

- ## Dark spots, blood spots or bloody ring around, or in the egg yolk

  The presence of blood clots or blood spots in an egg yolk is a possible sign of broken blood capillaries during the process of ovulation. A quail egg with such dark spots, blood spots or bloody ring around or in the egg yolk may be rightfully classified as abnormal.

- Abnormal color of the egg yolk

  The color of a normal egg yolk is supposed to be yellow. Any color deviation from this may be a sign of an abnormality.

- Unusual egg yolk

  The absence of an egg yolk or presence of double yolk in an egg would render such egg infertile and possibly unfit for human consumption.

Incubation

Question

How long should I store quail eggs before incubating them?

Answer

From my own experience, the hatching rate of the eggs is generally high at seven to eight days and below. Eggs older than seven days have a lower hatching rate. Significantly, eggs older than ten days tend to register minimal to sometimes nil hatching rate.

Question

What should be the ideal temperatures inside an incubator?

Answer

37.5^0c (99.5F) to 38^0C (100.5F). However, since each incubator is uniquely designed, you should always read the manufacturer's manual on how best to handle the incubator.

Question

How can I yield a high hatch rate using artificial egg incubator?

Answer

To guarantee a high hatch rate using artificial egg incubator, you should exercise the below:

- Use fertile eggs seven days old and below.
- Before putting the eggs inside an incubator, ensure they are clean, fresh and free from abnormalities (you can candle them to ascertain this).
- Put the eggs at room temperature for a few hours before putting them inside the incubator.
- Ensure the incubator is properly cleaned and disinfected (properly sterilized).
- Remember, for an incubator to hatch any egg effectively, it has to provide three things namely: *suitable temperature, relative humidity, and satisfactory amount of fresh air to the incubated egg.*
- Turn the eggs, three times each 24 hours to ensure uniform heating, except during the last two days to hatching (day 15 and onwards).

Question

What are the leading causes of poor egg hatch, and solutions for each case?

Answer

Below are the top five reasons for poor egg hatch, and possible solutions for each case.

Incubating infertile eggs

It can be a painful ordeal to stay optimistic in wait for chicks to hatch from incubated infertile eggs! In fact it would be miraculous should the infertile eggs hatch!

Solution

To help curb this, you should candle the eggs before presenting them for incubation. Again, once incubated, candle them – but before the 15th day of incubation to help detect infertile eggs. But going through the egg candling procedure, correctly pair the males and the females to guarantee high chances of fertility of the laid eggs.

Incubating abnormal eggs

As well outlined under egg candling, an egg may be classified as abnormal (an egg with a defect), if it has cracks on its outer shell, its shell is contaminated, has presence of double egg yolk, or absence of the yolk, or has very dark spots or blood ring around, or in its yolk. The chances of hatching fertile abnormal eggs are usually lower.

Solution

Again, before presenting the eggs for incubation, candle them to ensure that abnormal eggs or eggs with defects do not see the inside of an incubator. It's that simple!

Failure to turn the eggs/irregular turning of the eggs inside the incubator

The main reason for turning the eggs during incubation is to guarantee uniform heating of the incubated eggs. Failure to do so or irregular turning of the eggs may result into overheating of one side of the eggs, thus making them unreliable for hatching chicks.

Solution
During incubation, religiously, commit to turn the eggs, at least three times every twenty four hours. Equally, you can use an automatic egg incubator with a proven ability to urn the eggs at 180^0, at least three times each 24 hours.

Lack of favorable conditions inside the incubator

Remember, for a fertile egg to be hatched, the incubator has to provide: suitable temperature, relative humidity, and adequate amount of fresh air to the incubated egg. If the incubator you are using can't provide these three then be rest assured the incubated eggs will most probably fail to hatch.

Solution
As you incubate the eggs, always use incubators with proven potential to hatch eggs. Equally, if you reside in an area which experiences several power failures, you should have a power back up to stabilize the incubator during power blackouts.

The eggs may appear fertile when candled, but still fail to hatch chicks when incubated in the right incubator

Sometimes you may incubate fertile eggs using properly functioning incubator but still fail to realize hatching of the eggs.

Fertile eggs may fail to hatch due to a number of reasons such as incubating eggs from older breeds of quails or incubating eggs which have taken too long after being laid.

Solution
Always incubate eggs from younger but mature breeds of quails. Equally, incubate eggs which are utmost 7-8 days old and below. And most important, ensure the incubator is clean, disinfected and functioning well.

Raising Quail Chicks

What are the basic essentials inside a good brooder?

A good source of heat

A good source of heat is necessary to help heat up and regulate the temperature inside the brooder. Sources of heat may be in form of electric bulbs, gas burners, charcoal burners etc.

The brooder should be correctly heated all the time. The two best ways to verify this is by use of a thermometer, and or by closely watching behavior/movements/positions of the chicks around the heating source. If the chicks are crowding around the heating source, that's a sign for presence of cold in the incubator. But if they are hiding at the walls of the incubator (away from the heating source), that's a sign for too much heat in the brooder.

The temperature inside the brooder should be kept at 95F during the first week, and should thereafter be lowered by at least 5F on each passing week until the 4th week when the birds are ready to be taken out of the brooder.

When the brooder is correctly heated, the chicks should be evenly spread and will be seen normally going about their business. Gradually, withdraw the source of heat by the fourth week to allow the birds to adapt to the surrounding environment.

Litter

The main work of a litter inside a brooder is to help in keeping the brooder warm by absorbing wet moisture. The litter may be in form of sawdust, wood shavings, or paper cuttings. And since most quail chicks may have difficulty differentiating saw dust from their feeds, I prefer use of paper cuttings as bedding of the brooder. Already used litter should be timely discarded from the brooder to curb spread of contagious diseases like pneumonia and bad odor.

Waterers

The waterers should be set up in such a way that the chicks cannot step or defecate on them. The drinking water should be available in adequate portion, clean, fresh, and placed at convenient locations to avoid stressing the birds.

Fill the waterers with glass marbles or pebbles to bar the chicks from drowning in them. One of the leading causes of early mortality in quail chicks is by drowning in the waterers.

Don't forget to have the waterers cleaned thoroughly before filling up (you should clean them daily). And after two weeks, you can remove the glass marbles /pebbles from the drinking water.

Feeders

Clean and adequate feeders should be placed at convenient locations where chicks do not strain to access them. The feeders too, should be made in such a way that the chicks do not step or defecate on them.

Well-balanced feeds rich in protein should be readily available and given to the chicks at all times. As a good recommendation, you can feed them on game bird feeds /turkey feeds (a starter with an average protein component of 25%.

Once the birds are four weeks old, you should prepare to change their feeds to layers mash. By this time, you should have moved them to the cages. Most domesticated breeds of quail do start laying eggs at 6 weeks. Therefore, you should effectively change their feeds to layers mash as they approach the egg laying stage.

Enough ventilation

There should be adequate circulation of fresh air in the brooder. This is to allow for gaseous exchange and to keep contagious respiratory infections at bay.

Correct amount of light

The brooder should be correctly lit to allow the chicks to see the feeds and water. For small-scale, a heating bulb can as well serve the purpose of lighting the brooder and that of providing necessary heat.

Note

The brooder should be located at an ideal location away from noise and disturbance, and should securely built to protect the chicks from predators.

Equally, always exercise good grooming when handling the chicks, and ensure that they are raised under sanitary conditions.

Question

What's the best light to use inside a brooder housing 8-days old chicks and below?

Answer

You can use infrared heating bulb in such a brooder as it will both serve as a source of heat and light. Interestingly, infrared bulbs will equally not interfere with the sleeping patterns of the chicks inside the brooder.

Question

When is it appropriate to transfer chicks from the brooder to the cages?

Answer

Depending on their physical appearance, on the 3rd or 4th week, you should transfer the birds from the brooder to the cages, or to an appropriate housing.

Sexing

Question

How can I tell female quail from male quail?

Answer

Unless you have prior experience in handling quail, this might seem like some tricky puzzle to solve.

Given that there are various different types (breeds) of quails out there, being able to tell whether one is male or female can turn out to be a daunting task. However, it isn't supposed to be like that! There are various ways to use in distinguishing a male quail from a female one, and below are the four topmost ways:

By checking on the physical appearance

A number of female quails appear bigger in physical appearance when compared with their male counterparts of same breed and age. Summarily, the females will tend to appear slightly bigger than the males of the same breed and age.

By observing the color patterns on the birds' chests

Going this route is largely ideal for quails with speckled feathers like the Japanese quail. The female quails have speckled feathers on their chests while the male ones have plain feathered chests.

Examining quail's vent or cloaca

This is one of the most effective ways of distinguishing a male quail from a female one. There are two ways of examining the vent. First, when you press the area around it with your two fingers, a small ball-like lump may pop forward suggesting the bird is male. If the ball-like lump fails to show up then the bird is female.

Secondly, when you press the vent, you may see presence of some white foam coming out of it, suggesting the bird is male. You would not see the foam in females.

Roosting of the male birds

At five weeks, many breeds of male quail begin to roost (they begin to make some soft sound or noise). If you can patiently wait for the five weeks then you will have the perfect opportunity to be able to tell the male quails from the females from that roosting.

Question

How best should I pair my quail to guarantee high yield?

Answer

If all you want is fertile eggs, simply pair one male to utmost three females (though pairing of one male to two females usually yield far much better results). Such right pairing not only yields high fertility rate but equally prevents the hens from fighting over the male, or from fighting the male.

If all you want is unfertilized eggs, you should never be worried about how best to pair the birds. You can even keep all males and females separate from one another. You can equally mix the males and females, but this will yield some fertilized eggs.

Notably, the right pairing of the birds is key when you are after fertilized eggs.

Accommodation (Housing/Cages)

Where should I accommodate/house quail?

Use of Cages

Most of quail cages are specially built using wood and wire mesh. If you plan to house the birds in cages, a good recommendation is to use 2 sq ft per bird.

Construct the floor of the cages with wire mesh capable of easily letting the birds' droppings to fall off the cages. The mesh should equally be capable of barring predators from attacking quail.

There are two ways of acquiring the cages. First, you can buy already built cages from local dealers/breeders/suppliers, or secondly, you can build your own. When raising quails inside a cage, ensure the cages are roomy enough to avoid stressing the birds. Stressed birds are usually unproductive.

Use of a Coop / Pen or House

Here, quail are kept in a typical house-like structure, and are provided with necessities such as feeds, drinking water, a source of heat (for the chicks), and protection from predators.

Most people prefer to have quail pens or coops placed outdoors due to an ammonium-like smell contained in the birds' droppings.

If raised on the floor or solid ground, consider spreading wood shavings or sawdust. This makes cleaning of the birds' droppings from the coop to be easy. (With a spread of wood shavings on the floor, the droppings will be absorbed by the shavings to form dry crumbs which are easy to clean out of the accommodation).

In case you have any unutilized building in the farm, say like some shed or even a barn, you can turn it into a coop by covering it properly with recommended wire mesh. Doing so will help protect the birds from predators. The birds will equally lack any space to escape from the house.

Use of an aviary

An aviary is an enclosure with adequate space for the housed birds to move around freely. Interestingly, since quail have a cool personality, keeping them inside the aviary may result into lower egg production; especially if other birds are equally housed in the same aviary.

Also, due to the exposed nature of most aviaries, quail may be negatively affected by extreme temperatures; too hot or too cold temperatures may have adverse effects on their health.

On the other hand, a quail breed like the Chinese painted quail is a known aviary cleaner. It can comfortably feed on the feeds spilled on the floor of the aviary by other others. It will therefore help keep the aviary clean by feeding on food wastes, and in return, help you save on feed costs.

Note

In case you want to let quail to roam freely in any open field, clip their wings to prevent them from hopping away. Quails have a tendency to fly short distances and thus, can easily vanish if let in the open. In fact, many quail keepers have lost the birds due to releasing them in the open without properly clipping their wings.

Question

What's the best measurement of a wire to use in constructing quail cages?

Answer

¼ would be best ideal to use in constructing the floor of the cages, however, in certain instances, it may not effectively permit quails' droppings to pass through. Therefore, ½ would be appropriate. But as you settle on the ½, you must give consideration to the birds' predators which might be lurking in the area. One good way to bar the predators is by raising the cages from the ground, or putting metal barriers on the stands of the cages.

Question

Between an aviary and the cages, which one offers the best accommodation for raising quail?

Answer

If your desire is to raise the birds for production of eggs, meat, or for breeding purposes, raising them inside the cages would be ideal. But if your intention is to keep them for fun, as a hobby, or as domestic pets, you can consider raising them in an aviary.

Feeding

Question

Is it healthy to feed quail on chicken feeds?

Answer

First, it's important to note that quail are not poultry. They are game birds. Nonetheless, quail do comfortably feed on chicken feeds, but given that they are game birds, they need much higher protein content in their feeds as compared to chickens.

If you must give quail chicken feeds, ensure the feeds are supplemented with adequate relevant protein content. Significantly, quail chicks do need higher levels of protein in their diet (20-25%), to help them grow feathers and to put on good body weight.

If you therefore do the mistake of continuously feeding quail on un-supplemented chicken feeds (purely chicken feeds with minimal protein content), they could temporarily exhibit outward signs of a normal growth, but inwardly severely starving from the right amounts of proteins they vitally need.

Question

What quantity of feeds should I always put on the feeders?

Answer

As a precaution to avoid feed spillage, it is advisable to always half-fill the feeders at each refill. Nonetheless, quail are disciplined feeders and will know when to stop.

Question

What is the best recommendation for feeding quail? (From chicks to adult quails)

Answer

For your quail farming to remain a profitable venture, the birds must be well-fed on nutritious and well balanced feeds. The correct amount of feeding will allow the birds to give satisfactory output.

Due to their small body sizes, quail are adapted to consuming fewer amounts of feeds. Interestingly, they usually eat as much as they should. You should therefore never worry about any risk of overfeeding them. They know when to stop.

Quail need right feeds in right quantities to help them stay active and productive as they grow. Well balanced feeds assist their bodies to grow strong and develop immunity against possible attack poultry related diseases.

In case you buy quail chicks from a breeder or a quail farmer who doesn't take good care of the birds, ensure you feed the chicks on electrolytes and some warm water mixed with vitamins.

Below is a simple guide on feeding quail; from chicks to adult quail.

Use of Starter Feeds

Immediately the chicks are hatched, start them off with chick starter. Chick starters are usually rich in proteins which the chicks are in dire need of at that development stage.

Feed them on the starter feeds until they are 3-4 weeks old.

The protein content within the starter feeds usually varies. Notably, starter feeds for layers normally has higher levels of protein than the starter feeds for males.

As a good recommendation, you can feed them on game bird feeds /turkey feeds (a starter feed with an average protein content of 25%). However, at the start, you need to liaise with nearby trained and experienced quail farmers/breeders or poultry vets for recommendations on the best starter feeds that will best suit your quail breed.

Regular Feeds

Graduate the starter feeds to regular feeds when the birds attain 4 weeks. Put them on the starter feeds at between 4-6 weeks.

There are different regular feeds, or what others refer to as growers mash, for male quails (broilers) and for female quails (hens).

Ensure you get a good recommendation for the right growers mash from experienced quail bird farmers /breeders/ poultry vets (the names of these feeds differ from one country to another).

Take note that even at that stage, the starter feeds should still be constituted with a good percentage of proteins.

More Notes on feeding Quail

Did you know that quail can comfortably consume commercial chicken feeds? However, you should increase the protein content of commercial chicken feeds to be compatible with the high protein levels required by quail.

Since quail are known fussy eaters, you should buy quail feed pellets in mini sacks of say 25kgs each (in case you are keeping a few pairs of quails), as the feeds may go off before your quail feed on all of it

Non-medicated game bird feed is invaluably ideal to give to the birds as it rich in protein.

In the absence of commercial quail feed, the birds can be fed on soya meals, groundnut cakes, fish meals, sorghum, sunflower cakes, maize seeds (corn seeds), deoiled rice bran etc.

In addition to provision of quality feeds, do not forget to give the birds clean and fresh water for drinking. Equally, give them grit to help them improve on food digestion.

You can supplement their diet with kitchen scraps such as sweet corn, grated carrot, and broccoli, chunks of apple, lettuce, cut cabbages and even peas. You can also feed them on millet or mealworms.

Notably, mature males tend to shy off from eating mealworms. Instead, they present the mealworms to the hens as a sign of appreciation.

The more you feed quail on different feeds, the more you will learn about their favorite feeds.

Avoid feeding quail fresh cuttings from the garden as it is easy to mix in a poisonous plant. Equally, don't give them avocado or chocolate since the two are poisonous to a number of birds.

.

Quail Diseases
(Identification & Management)

How can I tell that my quail bird is sick?

Just like most poultry birds, sick quails may tend to exhibit some of the below characteristics:

- ## Numb, un-alert and unresponsive

  Sick quails may appear numb and un-alert. They may appear unresponsive to any form of touch, and will mostly be seen bored or sleeping within their accommodation. If standing, they will tend to exhibit an abnormal posture.

- ## Decline in egg production

  If there is a sudden drop in the number of eggs laid by the hens, that could a possible sign of disease infection within the flock.

- ## Extreme body temperatures

  You should occasionally check the body temperatures of the birds to establish if any could be exhibiting unusually high or unusually low temperature as such could be a sign of sickness.

- ## Lack of appetite

  Sick quails lack normal appetite and will resort to consuming reduced quantity of feeds.

- **Lackluster behavior**

  Sick quails may appear gloomy, and are largely uninterested even when you give them feeds or water.

- **Observable defects in defecations**

  When the defecation appears bloodstained, that could be a sure sign of internal infection. If it has an accompaniment of worms or larvae, that's a sign of possible parasitic infection. If it is hard, or watery, those could be signs of possible dehydration and diarrhea respectively.

- **Difficulty in breathing**

  Blocked mucus membranes, or any observable or hearable sound suggesting difficulty in breathing by bird could be a sign of respiratory infection, possibly pneumonia.

- **Rough or loose plumage**

  If the feathers are falling off, or appear rough in texture, be sure to check the bird closely for any possible disease or parasite infection.

Note

When you spot a bird exhibiting signs of sickness, isolate it from the rest of the flock, as fast as you possibly can. Afterwards, seek for the services of a trained and experienced poultry vet to help you diagnose and possibly treat the affected bird. Do not try to offer any form of treatment to a sick quail on your own if you aren't sure about the disease it might be suffering from. Things may turn tragic!

Question

What are the leading factors making quail to be susceptible to disease or pest infection?

Answer

Below are some of the most common predisposing factors to quail diseases.

- ## Age

  Did you know that older quail are usually prone to disease infections? This is due to their weakened body defense mechanisms. Equally, younger quails too are prone to infection by certain diseases due to their not-fully developed body immune system.

- ## Physical injuries

  Any physical injury inflicted on any part of a quail's body may make such wound susceptible to bacterial infection. Such injuries may be inflicted by other quail, quail owner, or even by the affected quail itself.

- ## Environment

  Very cold or very chilly weather conditions may make it possible for quail to contract respiratory diseases like pneumonia.

- ## Sex of quail

  Did you know that due to their frequencies in laying eggs, the egg laying birds are more delicate and more prone to disease infections as compared to roosters?

- ## Poor sanitation

  Unhygienic housing conditions may easily spur outbreak of certain contagious diseases like Coccidiosis.

- ## Mixing of other poultry breeds with quails

  This too may easily facilitate spread of contagious diseases within your flock. If say you mix quail and chickens in the same housing, any chicken suffering from a disease like histomoniasis may easily transmit it to quail.

Question

What are the best ways to deal with quail pests and diseases?

Answer

Below are some of the effective ways to help you deal with pests and diseases affecting quail

- Always raise the birds under sanitary conditions. The moment you choose to raise your birds negligently, under unsanitary conditions, be rest assured that when they fall sick and the best of drugs are administered, such drugs may be rendered ineffective. Raising quail under sanitary conditions is therefore your first step towards keeping healthy birds.

- Ensure the birds' house is always clean and properly disinfected. Wet and uncollected quails' droppings around water points and feeding zones may expose the birds to some deadly infections like Coccidiosis.

- Exercise timely dusting of the birds with appropriate pesticides to help keep external parasites away.

- Quail house should be well constructed to shield the birds from wind, hot sun, rodents like snakes, and other domestic pets like cats and dogs.

- Construct their house with cold insulators to keep the house warm during winter, and provide enough ventilation to cool down the house during hot summer. Equally, the house should have adequate exposure to light (natural or artificial).

- Always feed your flock on quality and well balanced diet. Purchase quail feeds and other feed containing the right amounts of nutrients needed by the birds. If done right, you should expect quality eggs and meat from your flock, coupled with hardy birds resistant to many diseases.

- Give the birds clean, fresh water for drinking, placed at strategic positions where they do not need any unnecessary strain to access to it. It is usually advisable to give them water at room temperature. Avoid giving them very cold or very hot water as they will avoid drinking such.

- The moment some quail begin to appear physically weak or gloomy, isolate them from the rest of the flock, as fast as you possibly can, and have them closely examined for any possible illness.

- De-worm the birds regularly using recommended de-wormers. This will aid in preventing infestations by worms and other protozoan diseases.

- De-beak any noted cannibal with the flock to bar them from inflicting wounds on other birds, which may subsequently make the wounded birds be susceptible to bacterial infections, or death.

Stress
(Causes and Management)

What are the leading causes of stress in quail?

Stress is any condition imposed on the birds making them to feel uncomfortable. Stress causes disturbance and may prevent quail from eating well, thus hindering their performance. Notably, stress may prevent female quail from laying eggs well.

Below are some of the most common causes of stress in quail:

- Sudden extreme temperatures (very hot or very cold temperatures).
- Sudden change in routine, i.e. sudden change in type of feeds, feed locations, location of waterers etc.
- Sudden loud noises like thunderstorm, loud music, noisy automobiles, low flying planes etc.
- Insufficient/lack of adequate feeds and water.
- Presence of strangers, pests and predators within quails' accommodation.
- When new birds are introduced in the old flock..
- Improper handling of birds i.e. improper handling during culling or during vaccination.
- Overcrowding in the quails' house forcing the birds to compete for space, feeds and water.

Question

What are the most effective ways of dealing with stress in quail?

Answer

Below are some practices you can consider adopting to help you manage stress in quail:

- If you must change any daily routine, like time of re-filling feeders etc., do it gradually.
- Control any pests or diseases which may be affecting the birds.
- Properly insulate quail house to guarantee uniform temperature throughout the year.
- Protect the birds from loud noise.
- Gradually, introduce new birds to the old flock.
- Minimize access of quail house by strangers.
- Keep the correct number of birds per housing unit whilst ensuring they have adequate provision of balanced feeds and water.
- Handle the birds rightly during culling, during vaccination, or when moving them from one point to another.

Vices
(Causes and Management)

What are vices, and what are the leading causes of vices in quail?

Answer

Vices are bad habits that quail may develop due to their environmental exposure. The two most common quail vices are egg eating, and cannibalism.

Below are some of the most common factors which may expose quails to develop vices.

- Idleness. An idle quail can easily turn destructive.
- Broken or soft-shelled eggs may tempt the birds to want to peck them.
- Any delay in collection of laid eggs may tempt the birds to peck them.
- Quail lacking minerals such as calcium and phosphorus may force the affected birds to peck for them elsewhere.
- Overcrowding in the quails' house may force some hens to lay eggs on areas where other birds can easily access them and possibly try to peck them.
- Still, overcrowding may encourage some birds to peck one another, possibly in hope of removing external pests from one another.

- Introduction of new birds with bad habits into an old flock with no known bad habits may tempt the old birds to pick up such bad habits.

- Mixing quail of different age groups may expose birds of younger age to bullying by adult quail.

- In case quail are laying eggs in a nesting box, any presence of bright light in the laying nests may expose the laid eggs to pecking.

- Immediately a female quail lays an egg and then starts to move around even before its cloaca retracts (for female quail with disorders such as prolapsed vent), this might excite other birds to want to peck the unretracted cloaca.

Question

What are the most effective ways of controlling vices in quail?

Answer

Below are some measures you can take to help you manage vices in quails:

- Keep the birds busy all the time by giving them green vegetables hanged at the right height within their accommodation. The vegetables or greens should be free from sprays of pesticides.

- Keep the light around or within the laying nests at minimum so that the birds may not easily notice the laid eggs.

- Collect eggs frequently from the nests, two to three times each 24 hours.

- Cull and, or debeak any noted cannibal within the flock.

- Cull hens with prolapsed vent; those whose cloaca takes time before retracting - to avoid tempting other birds to peck them.

- Provide the birds with well-balanced and nutritious feeds, containing all the necessary nutrients and minerals they need.

- Keep the birds according to their age groups to help thwart bullying of younger birds by birds of older age.

- Keep the correct number of birds per housing unit; with adequate balanced feeds and waterers provided.

- Dust the birds regularly to contain attack and spread of external pests and parasites.

It is often affirmed that prevention is better than cure. It can turn out costly to expose quail to diseases which can easily be prevented. Once quail are infected by any disease, the two possible outcomes are: Losing them to the disease, or incurring costly expenses on their treatments or medications.

General Questions And Answers

Question

Is it illegal to keep quail without relevant approvals?

Answer

Did you know that at one point in history, quails almost became extinct? Therefore, to preserve and increase their numbers across the world, most countries and governments do classify them as endangered wild birds. They then provide for their protection through certain legislations. If you reside in a country where such quail related legislations do exist, then do the right thing: get the relevant approvals before keeping the birds.

You can never play a hide-and-seek game with the government or with authorities forever. You can be lucky in one incident, but not forever! In fact, there is a common saying in my country that '*the Government has long arms*'. In the event you decide to raise quail without following due process or without relevant approvals, be rest assured it won't take long before being caught. And you can guess what might happen when you are caught!

Question

My bird has just left a huge dropping in the evening/morning, should I be worried?

Answer

First, check if there could be any observable defects in the droppings like blood stains, or presence of any parasites such as worms or larvae. If there is none then you should have no cause for alarm. Such birds might have just taken too long before releasing the droppings. Equally, if it is a hen, then it could possibly be exhibiting broody-signs.

Question

What is the difference between button quail (Chinese painted quail) and buttonquails (hemipodes)?

Answer

Buttonquails may physically appear to resemble quails, but are genetically unrelated to quails. The Chinese painted quails fall in the family of Phasianidae of order of Galliformes, while buttonquails (hemipodes) on the other hand are a small family of birds falling in the family of Turnicidae of the order of Charadriiformes.

Question

What do I need to effectively raise healthy quails?

Answer

Below are the four vital essentials you'll need to help you raise healthy birds:

1. **Go through lots of relevant and up-to-date information on quails and quail farming**.

It's essential to know what you are getting into and how best you will effectively stay in it. It's that simple! Dig deep on quails and quail farming. Have enough relevant information on the latest developments in the quail farming industry, plus general market trends in the poultry farming segment. Afterwards, secure all the legal documents, if necessary, to guarantee noninterference from authorities or neighbors once you start keeping the birds.

The more information you know on quails and quail farming, the more effective you will be at raising the birds.

2. **Have the right breeds from the start, depending on your purpose for keeping the birds.**

There is an old adage in the poultry world that if you start with a desirable breed, you should anticipate desirable output. But if you start with an undesirable breed, anticipate undesirable output. The quality of input is directly proportional to the quality of output. In summary, if you want to raise the birds for purposes of egg or meat production, get the right breeds with proven high yield potential. Don't try re-inventing the wheel.

3. **Have a correct housing facility, or a secure space for safe rearing of quails**

Whether you are raising the birds for domestic or commercial ends, on large scale or small scale, in cages or via free-range system, know quails thrive best where there is minimal distraction. Raise them in the right housing, with the right number of birds per unit – avoid overcrowding them. The housing should be located in a secure place with limited access to strangers, and no access to rodents. The location should be noise-free to encourage maximum yield.

4. **Know about quail feeds and best quail disease management practices**

To effectively raise healthy quail, you must arm yourself with the right knowledge on quail feeds and best disease management practices. This can never be overemphasized. In case you feel disadvantaged with such information or knowledge, it is advisable to readily seek for the services of trained and experienced quail professionals within your location.

Question

What should I do to ensure I get the correct breeding flock for my quail farming venture?

Answer

The type of breeding flock you start out with will determine the quality of gains from your quail farming venture. Therefore, you need to be really keen when selecting your initial flock of quail chicks.

The following five tips should help you in making a decision when purchasing your initial flock for raising.

- Visit at least two different quail farms or quail keepers to see how they are taking care of the birds. This will give you an opportunity to foresee what awaits you.

- Are there licensed or reputable quail breeders or quail related dealer outlets within your region? These are the very first entities you should give first preference when you decide to buy your first flock. Aim to start out with the best performing breeds available from them.

- Avoid purchase of flock with deformities or those of different sizes and different colors - they will most probably not get along, resulting into low output.

- Establish history of mortality or disease history of the birds you intend to purchase. Most breeders or dealers have these records in their possessions.

- If you decide to purchase eggs for incubation purposes, get eggs with equal (similar) sizes, shapes and colors.

Question

What is the best quail breed to consider raising?

Answer

The best quail breed to consider raising is largely dependent on your need or purpose for keeping quail. Many different people keep different breeds of quail for different reasons. Some of the top reasons why many people keep quail include provision of eggs, meat, both eggs and meat, as domestic pets, for commercial gains, etc.

Notably, different quail breeds have different personalities. Before you settle on raising any quail breed, simply carry out adequate research on your need for keeping the birds, and the type of personality you would want the birds to exhibit.

You can visit a few established quail farmers or quail breeders to have that invaluable firsthand experience on which best breed would suit your need. Significantly, as a beginner, the best quail breed to consider raising should be both locally and readily available.

THE END

Made in the USA
Monee, IL
14 March 2023